Lean and Green Cookbook

Enjoy amazing food without feeling hungry, everyday new lean and green recipes to help you stay healthy and lose weight

Nichole S. Rodriguez

Table of contents

—

5

—

6

INRODUCTION

The lean green diet is the same as the green diet, except that it makes use of lean protein sources instead of high-fat ones.

In general, lean protein sources include skinless poultry, fish (e.g. cod and haddock), lean cuts of meat, eggs, and vegetable proteins such as lentils and beans.

Some may think that the low-fat diet is better for everyone when it comes to losing weight and improving health than a conventional low-fat diet, but the evidence does not yet support this claim. Recent studies show that low-fat diets have similar results to low-fat diets in reducing body weight. Furthermore, they do not show a considerable improvement in health risk factors such as blood lipids, blood pressure, and insulin resistance compared to low-fat diets.

The lean green diet is a special variant of the low-fat diet, which makes additional use of lean protein instead of fat in promoting weight loss and improving health risk. Lean protein sources include skinless poultry, fish (e.g. cod and haddock), lean cuts of meat, eggs, and vegetable proteins such as lentils and beans. This type of diet improves metabolism by increasing the metabolic rate, which accelerates weight loss. It also reduces the risk of *obesity, because following the Lean Green Diet does not put on as much weight as low-fat diets.*

The emphasis is on eating a small amount of meat and fish twice a day, along with other sources of protein such as eggs, lentils, and beans. The diet includes vegetables as well as vitamin-rich fruits (e.g. carrots). Green food includes different varieties of beans such as green lentils, black peas, and soybeans.

The lean and green diet is one of the healthy diets that should be consumed frequently because it is complimentary. The pros of the lean green diet are that it does not increase the risk of obesity, reduces body weight, and improves health. The cons of the lean green diet are that it is not very popular and not many people know about it. On the other hand, the lean and green diet is a healthy variant of the low-fat diet that is low in fat, high in fiber, and rich in nutrients such as vitamins B6, B12, and C. It should be consumed by everyone who wants to follow a healthy diet plan

BREAKFAST RECIPES

Avocado Red Peppers Roasted Scrambled Eggs

Preparation Time: 10 minutes

Cooking Time: 12 minutes

Servings: 3

Ingredients:

- *1/2 tablespoon butter*

- *Eggs, 2*

- *1/2 roasted red pepper, about 1 1/2 ounces*

- *1/2 small avocado, coarsely chopped, about 2 1/4 ounces*

- *Salt, to taste*

Directions:

1. *In a nonstick skillet, heat the butter over medium heat. Break the eggs into the pan and break the yolks with a spoon. Sprinkle with a little salt.*

2. *Stir to stir and continue stirring until the eggs start to come out. Quickly add the bell peppers and avocado.*

3. *Cook and stir until the eggs suit your taste. Adjust the seasoning, if necessary.*

Nutrition: Calories: 317 Fat: 26g Protein: 14g Dietary Fiber: 5g Net Carbs: 4g

Mushroom Quickie Scramble

Preparation Time: *10 minutes*

Cooking Time: *10 minutes*

Servings: *4*

Ingredients:

- *3 small-sized eggs, whisked*

- *4 pcs. Bella mushrooms*

- *½ cup of spinach*

- *¼ cup of red bell peppers*

- *2 deli ham slices*

- *1 tablespoon of ghee or coconut oil*

- *Salt and pepper to taste*

Directions:

1. *Chop the ham and veggies.*

2. *Put half a tbsp. of butter in a frying pan and heat until melted.*

3. *Sauté the ham and vegetables in a frying pan then set aside.*

4. Get a new frying pan and heat the remaining butter.

5. Add the whisked eggs into the second pan while stirring continuously to avoid overcooking.

6. When the eggs are done, sprinkle with salt and pepper to taste.

7. Add the ham and veggies to the pan with the eggs.

8. Mix well.

9. Remove from burner and transfer to a plate.

Nutrition: Calories: 350 Total Fat: 29 g Protein: 21 g Total Carbs: 5 g

Coconut Coffee and Ghee

Preparation Time: *10 minutes*

Cooking Time: *10 minutes*

Servings: *5*

Ingredients:

- *½ Tbsp. of coconut oil*

- *½ Tbsp. of ghee*

- *1 to 2 cups of preferred coffee (or rooibos or black tea, if preferred)*

- *1 Tbsp. of coconut or almond milk*

Directions:

1. *Place the almond (or coconut) milk, coconut oil, ghee, and coffee in a blender (or milk frother).*

2. *Mix for around 10 seconds or until the coffee turns creamy and foamy.*

3. *Pour contents into a coffee cup.*

4. *Serve immediately and enjoy.*

Nutrition: *Calories: 150 Total Fat: 15 g Protein: 0 g Total Carbs: 0 g Net Carbs: 0 g*

Yummy Veggie Waffles

Preparation Time: 10 minutes

Cooking Time: 9 minutes

Servings: 3

Ingredients:

- *3 cups raw cauliflower, grated*
- *1 cup cheddar cheese*
- *1 cup mozzarella cheese*
- *½ cup parmesan*
- *1/3 cup chives, finely sliced*
- *6 eggs*
- *1 teaspoon garlic powder*
- *1 teaspoon onion powder*
- *½ teaspoon chili flakes*
- *Dash of salt and pepper*

Directions:

1. *Turn waffle maker on.*
2. *In a bowl, mix all the listed ingredients very well until incorporated.*

3. *Once the waffle maker is hot, distribute the waffle mixture into the insert.*

4. *Let cook for about 9 minutes, flipping at 6 minutes.*

5. *Remove from waffle maker and set aside.*

6. *Serve and enjoy!*

Nutrition: Calories: 390 Fat: 28 g Carbs: 6 g Fiber: 2 g Protein: 30 g

Omega 3 Breakfast Shake

Preparation Time: 5 minutes

Cooking Time: 5 minutes

Servings: 2

Ingredients:

- 1 cup vanilla almond milk (unsweetened)
- 2 tablespoons blueberries
- 1 ½ tablespoons flaxseed meal
- 1 tablespoon MCT Oil
- ¾ tablespoon banana extract
- ½ tablespoon chia seeds
- 5 drops Stevia (liquid form)
- 1/8 tablespoon Xanthan gum

Directions:

1. In a blender, mix vanilla almond milk, banana extract, Stevia, and three ice cubes.

2. When smooth, add blueberries and pulse.

3. Once blueberries are thoroughly incorporated, add flaxseed meal and chia seeds.

4. *Let sit for 5 minutes.*

5. *After 5 minutes, pulse again until all ingredients are nicely distributed. Serve and enjoy*

Nutrition: Calories: 264 Fats: 25 g Carbs: 7 g Protein: 4 g

Lime Bacon Thyme Muffins

Preparation Time: 10 minutes

Cooking Time: 20 minutes

Servings: 3

Ingredients:

- *3 cups of almond flour*
- *4 medium-sized eggs*
- *1 cup of bacon bits*
- *2 tsp. of lemon thyme*
- *½ cup of melted ghee*
- *1 tsp. of baking soda*
- *½ tsp. of salt, to taste*

Directions:

1. *Pre-heat oven to 3500 F.*
2. *Put ghee in mixing bowl and melt.*
3. *Add baking soda and almond flour.*
4. *Put the eggs in.*

5. Add the lemon thyme (if preferred, other herbs or spices may be used).

6. Drizzle with salt.

7. Mix all ingredients well.

8. Sprinkle with bacon bits

9. Line the muffin pan with liners.

10. Spoon mixture into the pan, filling the pan to about ¾ full.

11. Bake for about 20 minutes. Test by inserting a toothpick into a muffin. If it comes out clean, then the muffins are done.

Nutrition: Calories: 300 Total Fat: 28 g Protein: 11 g Total Carbs: 6 g Fiber: 3 g

Pizza Hack

Preparation Time: 5-10 minutes

Cooking Time: 15-20 minutes

Servings: 1

Ingredients:

- *1/4 fueling of garlic mashed potato*

- *1/2 egg whites*

- *1/4 tablespoon of baking powder*

- *3/4 oz. of reduced-fat shredded mozzarella*

- *1/8 cup of sliced white mushrooms*

- *1/16 cup of pizza sauce*

- *3/4 oz. of ground beef*

- *1/4 sliced black olives*

- *You also need a sauté pan, baking sheets, and parchment paper*

Directions:

1. *Start by preheating the oven to 400°.*

2. *Mix your baking powder and garlic potato packet.*

3. *Add egg whites to your mixture and stir well until it blends.*

4. *Line the baking sheet with parchment paper and pour the mixed batter onto it.*

5. *Put another parchment paper on top of the batter and spread out the batter to a 1/8-inch circle.*

6. *Then place another baking sheet on top; this way, the batter is between two baking sheets.*

7. *Place into an oven and bake for about 8 minutes until the pizza crust is golden brown.*

8. *For the toppings, place your ground beef in a sauté pan and fry till it's brown and wash your mushrooms very well.*

9. *After the crust is baked, remove the top layer of parchment paper carefully to prevent the foam from sticking to the pizza crust.*

10. *Put your toppings on top of the crust and bake for an extra 8 minutes.*

11. *Once ready, slide the pizza off the parchment paper and onto a plate.*

Nutrition: Calories: 478 Protein: 30 g Carbohydrates: 22 g Fats: 29 g

Amaranth Porridge

Preparation Time: 5 minutes

Cooking Time: 30 minutes

Servings: 2.

Ingredients:

- *2 cups coconut milk*

- *2 cups alkaline water*

- *1 cup amaranth*

- *2 tbsps. coconut oil*

- *1 tbsp. ground cinnamon*

Directions:

1. *In a saucepan, mix in the milk with water, then boil the mixture.*

2. *You stir in the amaranth, then reduce the heat to medium.*

3. *Cook on the medium heat, then simmer for at least 30 minutes as you stir it occasionally.*

4. *Turn off the heat.*

5. *Add in cinnamon and coconut oil then stir.*

6. Serve.

Nutrition: Calories: 434 kcal Fat: 35g Carbs: 27g Protein: 6.7g

Sweet Cashew Cheese Spread

Preparation Time: *5 minutes*

Cooking Time: *5 minutes*

Servings: *10 servings*

Ingredients:

- *Stevia (5 drops)*

- *Cashews (2 cups, raw)*

- *Water (1/2 cup)*

Directions:

1. *Soak the cashews overnight in water.*

2. *Next, drain the excess water then transfer cashews to a food processor.*

3. *Add in the stevia and the water.*

4. *Process until smooth.*

5. *Serve chilled. Enjoy.*

Nutrition: Fat: 7 g Cholesterol: 0 mg Sodium: 12.6 mg Carbohydrates: 5.7 g

Mini Zucchini Bites

Preparation Time: 10 minutes

Cooking Time: 10 minutes

Servings: 6

Ingredients:

- *1 zucchini, cut into thick circles*

- *3 cherry tomatoes, halved*

- *1/2 cup parmesan cheese, grated*

- *Salt and pepper to taste*

- *1 tsp. chives, chopped*

Directions:

1. *Preheat the oven to 390 degrees F.*

2. *Add wax paper on a baking sheet.*

3. *Arrange the zucchini pieces.*

4. *Add the cherry halves on each zucchini slice.*

5. *Add parmesan cheese, chives, and sprinkle with salt and pepper.*

6. *Bake for 10 minutes. Serve.*

Nutrition: Fat: 1.0 g Cholesterol: 5.0 mg Sodium: 400.3 mg Potassium: 50.5 mg Carbohydrates

Gluten-Free Pancakes

Preparation Time: 5 minutes

Cooking Time: 2 minutes

Servings: 2

Ingredients:

- *6 eggs*
- *1 cup low-fat cream cheese*
- *1 1/12; teaspoons baking powder*
- *1 scoop protein powder*
- *1/4 cup almond meal*
- *¼ teaspoon salt*

Directions:

1. *Combine dry ingredients in a food processor. Add the eggs one after another and then the cream cheese. Mix it well.*

2. *Lightly grease a skillet with cooking spray and place over medium-high heat.*

3. *Pour the batter into the pan. Turn the pan gently to create round pancakes.*

4. *Cook for about 2 minutes on each side.*

5. Serve pancakes with your favorite topping.

Nutrition: Dietary Fiber: 1 g Net Carbs: 5 g Protein: 25 g Total Fat: 14 g Calories: 288

Mushroom & Spinach Omelet

Preparation Time: 20 minutes

Cooking Time: 20 minutes

Servings: 3

Ingredients:

- 2 tablespoons butter, divided
- 6-8 fresh mushrooms, sliced, 5 ounces
- Chives, chopped, optional
- Salt and pepper, to taste
- 1 handful baby spinach, about 1/2 ounce
- Pinch garlic powder
- 4 eggs, beaten
- 1-ounce shredded Swiss cheese

Directions:

1. In a very large saucepan, sauté the mushrooms in one tablespoon of butter until soft. Season with salt, pepper, and garlic.

2. Remove the mushrooms from the pan and keep warm. Heat the remaining tablespoon of butter in the same skillet over medium heat.

3. *Beat the eggs with a little salt and pepper and add to the hot butter. Turn the pan over to coat the entire bottom of the pan with egg. Once the egg is almost out, place the cheese over the middle of the tortilla.*

4. *Fill the cheese with spinach leaves and hot mushrooms. Let cook for about a minute for the spinach to start to wilt. Fold the empty side of the tortilla carefully over the filling and slide it onto a plate and sprinkle with chives, if desired.*

5. *Alternatively, you can make two tortillas using half the mushroom, spinach, and cheese filling in each.*

Nutrition: Calories: 321 Fat: 26 g Protein: 19 g Carbohydrate: 4 g Dietary Fiber: 1 g

LUNCH RECIPES

Yummy Smoked Salmon

Preparation Time: 10 minutes

Cooking Time: 10 minutes

Servings: 3

Ingredients:

- *4 eggs; whisked*
- *1/2 teaspoon avocado oil*
- *4 ounces smoked salmon; chopped.*

For the sauce:

- *1/2 cup cashews; soaked; drained*
- *1/4 cup green onions; chopped.*
- *1 teaspoon garlic powder*
- *1 cup coconut milk*
- *1 tablespoon lemon juice*
- *Salt and black pepper to the taste.*

Directions:

1. *In your blender, mix cashews with coconut milk, garlic powder and lemon juice and blend well.*
2. *Add salt, pepper and green onions, blend again well, transfer to a bowl and keep in the fridge for now.*
3. *Heat up a pan with the oil over medium-low heat; add eggs, whisk a bit and cook until they are almost done*

4. *Introduce in your preheated broiler and cook until eggs set.*

5. *Divide eggs on plates, top with smoked salmon and serve with the green onion sauce on top.*

Nutrition: Calories: 200 Fat: 10 Fiber: 2 Carbs: 11 Protein:

Almond Coconut Cereal

Preparation Time: 5 minutes

Cooking Time: 5 minutes

Servings: 2

Ingredients:

- *Water, 1/3 cup.*
- *Coconut milk, 1/3 cup.*
- *Roasted sunflower seeds, 2 tbsps.*
- *Chia seeds, 1 tbsp.*
- *Blueberries, ½ cup.*
- *Chopped almonds, 2 tbsps.*

Directions:

1. *Set a medium bowl in position to add coconut milk and chia seeds then reserve for five minutes*
2. *Plug in and set the blender in position to blend almond with sunflower seeds*
3. *Stir the combination to chia seeds mixture then add water to mix evenly.*
4. *Serve topped with the remaining sunflower seeds and blueberries*

Nutrition: Calories: 181 Fat: 15.2 Fiber: 4 Carbs: 10.8 Protein: 3.7

Almond Porridge

Preparation Time: 10 minutes

Cooking Time: 5 minutes

Servings: 1

Ingredients:

- Ground cloves, ¼ tsp.
- Nutmeg, ¼ tsp.
- Stevia, 1 tsp.
- Coconut cream, ¾ cup.
- Ground almonds, ½ cup.
- Ground cardamom, ¼ tsp.
- Ground cinnamon, 1 tsp.

Directions:

1. Set your pan over medium heat to cook the coconut cream for a few minutes
2. Stir in almonds and stevia to cook for 5 minutes
3. Mix in nutmeg, cardamom, and cinnamon
4. Enjoy while still hot

Nutrition: Calories: 695 Fat: 66.7 Fiber: 11.1 Carbs: 22 Protein: 14.3

Asparagus Frittata Recipe

Preparation Time: 20 minutes

Cooking Time: 20 minutes

Servings: 4

Ingredients:

- Bacon slices, chopped: 4
- Salt and black pepper
- Eggs (whisked): 8
- Asparagus (trimmed and chopped): 1 bunch

Directions:

1. Heat a pan, add bacon, stir and cook for 5 minutes.
2. Add asparagus, salt, and pepper, stir and cook for another 5 minutes.
3. Add the chilled eggs, spread them in the pan, let them stand in the oven and bake for 20 minutes at 350° F.
4. Share and divide between plates and serve for breakfast.

Nutrition: Calories 251 Carbs 16 Fat 6 Fiber 8 Protein 7

Avocados Stuffed with Salmon

Preparation Time: 5 minutes

Cooking Time: 5 minutes

Servings: 2

Ingredients:

- *Avocado (pitted and halved): 1*
- *Olive oil: 2 tablespoons*
- *Lemon juice: 1*
- *Smoked salmon (flaked): 2 ounces*
- *Goat cheese (crumbled): 1 ounce*
- *Salt and black pepper*

Directions:

1. *Combine the salmon with lemon juice, oil, cheese, salt, and pepper in your food processor and pulsate well.*
2. *Divide this mixture into avocado halves and serve.*
3. *Dish and Enjoy!*

Nutrition: Calories: 300 Fat: 15 Fiber: 5 Carbs: 8 Protein: 16

Bacon and Brussels Sprout Breakfast

Preparation Time: *10 minutes*

Cooking Time: *15 minutes*

Servings: *3*

Ingredients:

- Apple cider vinegar, 1½ tbsps.
- Salt
- Minced shallots, 2
- Minced garlic cloves, 2
- Medium eggs, 3
- Sliced Brussels sprouts, 12 oz.
- Black pepper
- Chopped bacon, 2 oz.
- Melted butter, 1 tbsp.

Directions:

1. Over medium heat, quick fry the bacon until crispy then reserve on a plate
2. Set the pan on fire again to fry garlic and shallots for 30 seconds
3. Stir in apple cider vinegar, Brussels sprouts, and seasoning to cook for five minutes
4. Add the bacon to cook for five minutes then stir in the butter and set a hole at the center

5. Crash the eggs to the pan and let cook fully

6. Enjoy

Nutrition: Calories: 275 Fat: 16.5 Fiber: 4.3 Carbs: 17.2 Protein: 17.4

Bacon and Lemon spiced Muffins

Preparation Time: 10 minutes

Cooking Time: 20 minutes

Servings: 12

Ingredients:

- Lemon thyme, 2 tsps.
- Salt
- Almond flour, 3 cup.
- Melted butter, ½ cup.
- Baking soda, 1 tsp.
- Black pepper
- Medium eggs, 4
- Diced bacon, 1 cup.

Directions:

1. Set a mixing bowl in place and stir in the eggs and baking soda to incorporate well.
2. Whisk in the seasonings, butter, bacon, and lemon thyme
3. Set the mixture in a well-lined muffin pan.
4. Set the oven for 20 minutes at 3500F, allow to bake
5. Allow the muffins to cool before serving

Nutrition: Calories: 186 Fat: 17.1 Fiber: 0.8 Carbs: 1.8 Protein: 7.4

Tropical Greens Smoothie

Preparation Time: 5 Minutes

Cooking Time: 0 Minutes

Servings: 1

Ingredients:

- One banana

- 1/2 large navel orange, peeled and segmented

- 1/2 cup frozen mango chunks

- 1 cup frozen spinach

- One celery stalk, broken into pieces

- One tablespoon cashew butter or almond butter

- 1/2 tablespoon spiraling

- 1/2 tablespoon ground flaxseed

- 1/2 cup unsweetened nondairy milk

- Water, for thinning (optional)

Directions:

1. In a high-speed blender or food processor, combine the bananas, orange, mango, spinach, celery, cashew butter, spiraling (if using), flaxseed, and milk.

2. Blend until creamy, adding more milk or water to thin the smoothie if too thick. Serve immediately—it is best served fresh.

Nutrition: Calories: 391 Fat: 12g Protein: 13g Carbohydrates: 68g Fiber: 13g

Vitamin C Smoothie Cubes

Preparation Time: 5 minutes

Cooking Time: 8 hours to chill

Servings: 1

Ingredients:

- 1/8 large papaya

- 1/8 mango

- 1/4 cups chopped pineapple, fresh or frozen

- 1/8 cup raw cauliflower florets, fresh or frozen

- 1/4 large navel oranges, peeled and halved

- 1/4 large orange bell pepper stemmed, seeded, and coarsely chopped

Directions:

1. Halve the papaya and mango, remove the pits, and scoop their soft flesh into a high-speed blender.

2. *Add the pineapple, cauliflower, oranges, and bell pepper. Blend until smooth.*

3. *Evenly divide the puree between 2 (16-compartment) ice cube trays and place them on a level surface in your freezer. Freeze for at least 8 hours.*

4. *The cubes can be left in the ice cube trays until use or transferred to a freezer bag. The frozen cubes are good for about three weeks in a standard freezer, or up to 6 months in a chest freezer.*

Nutrition: Calories: 96 Fat: 1 g Protein: 2 g Carbohydrates: 24 g Fiber: 4 g

Overnight Chocolate Chia Pudding

Preparation Time: 2 minutes

Cooking Time: overnight to chill

Servings: 1

Ingredients:

- *1/8 cup chia seeds*
- *1/2 cup unsweetened nondairy milk*
- *One tablespoon raw cocoa powder*
- *1/2 teaspoon vanilla extract*
- *1/2 teaspoon pure maple syrup*

Directions:

1. *Stir together the chia seeds, milk, cacao powder, vanilla, and maple syrup in a large bowl.*
2. *Divide between two (1/2-pint) covered glass jars or containers.*
3. *Refrigerate overnight.*
4. *Stir before serving.*

Nutrition: Calories: 213 Fat: 10 g Protein: 9 g Carbohydrates: 20 g Fiber: 15 g

Slow Cooker Savory Butternut Squash Oatmeal

Preparation Time: 15 minutes

Cooking Time: 6 to 8 hours

Servings: 1

Ingredients:

- *1/4 cup steel-cut oats*

- *1/2 cups cubed (1/2-inch pieces), peeled butternut squash (freeze any leftovers after preparing a whole squash for future meals)*

- *3/4 cups of water*

- *1/16 cup unsweetened nondairy milk*

- *1/4 tablespoon chia seeds*

- *1/2 teaspoons yellow miso paste*

- *3/4 teaspoons ground ginger*

- *1/4 tablespoon sesame seeds, toasted*

- *1/4 tablespoon chopped scallion, green parts only*

- *Shredded carrot, for serving (optional)*

Directions:

1. In a slow cooker, combine the oats, butternut squash, and water.

2. Cover the slow cooker and cook on low for 6 to 8 hours, or until the squash is fork-tender.

3. Using a potato masher or heavy spoon, roughly mash the cooked butternut squash.

4. Stir to combine with the oats.

5. Whisk together the milk, chia seeds, miso paste, and ginger in a large bowl. Stir the mixture into the oats.

6. Top your oatmeal bowl with sesame seeds and scallion for more plant-based fiber, top with shredded carrot (if using).

Nutrition: Calories: 230 Fat: 5 g Protein: 7 g Carbohydrates: 40 g Fiber: 9 g

DINNER RECIPES

Pork and Peppers Chili

Preparation Time: 5 minutes

Cooking Time: 8 hours 5 minutes

Servings: 4

Ingredients:

- 1 red onion, chopped
- 2 pounds' pork, ground
- 4 garlic cloves, minced
- 2 red bell peppers, chopped
- 1 celery stalk, chopped
- 25 ounces' fresh tomatoes, peeled, crushed
- ¼ cup green chilies, chopped
- 2 tablespoons fresh oregano, chopped
- 2 tablespoons chili powder
- A pinch of salt and black pepper
- A drizzle of olive oil

Directions:

1. Heat up a sauté pan with the oil over medium-high heat and add the onion, garlic and the meat. Mix and brown for 5 minutes then transfer to your slow cooker.
2. Add the rest of the ingredients, toss, cover and cook on low for 8 hours.

3. Divide everything into bowls and serve.

Nutrition: Calories 448 Fat 13 Fiber 6.6 Carbs 20.2 Protein 63g

Greek Style Quesadillas

Preparation Time: 10 minutes

Cooking Time: 10 minutes

Servings: 4

Ingredients:

- 4 whole wheat tortillas
- 1 cup Mozzarella cheese, shredded
- 1 cup fresh spinach, chopped
- 2 tablespoon Greek yogurt
- 1 egg, beaten
- ¼ cup green olives, sliced
- 1 tablespoon olive oil
- 1/3 cup fresh cilantro, chopped

Directions:

1. In the bowl, combine together Mozzarella cheese, spinach, yogurt, egg, olives, and cilantro.
2. Then pour olive oil in the skillet.
3. Place one tortilla in the skillet and spread it with Mozzarella mixture.
4. Top it with the second tortilla and spread it with cheese mixture again.

5. Then place the third tortilla and spread it with all remaining cheese mixture.
6. Cover it with the last tortilla and fry it for 5 minutes from each side over the medium heat.

Nutrition: Calories 193 Fat 7.7 Fiber 3.2 Carbs 23.6 Protein 8.3

Creamy Penne

Preparation Time: 10 minutes

Cooking Time: 25 minutes

Servings: 4

Ingredients:

- ½ cup penne, dried
- 9 oz. chicken fillet
- 1 teaspoon Italian seasoning
- 1 tablespoon olive oil
- 1 tomato, chopped
- 1 cup heavy cream
- 1 tablespoon fresh basil, chopped
- ½ teaspoon salt
- 2 oz. Parmesan, grated
- 1 cup water, for cooking

Directions:

1. Pour water in the pan, add penne, and boil it for 15 minutes. Then drain water.

2. *Pour olive oil in the skillet and heat it up.*
3. *Slice the chicken fillet and put it in the hot oil.*
4. *Sprinkle chicken with Italian seasoning and roast for 2 minutes from each side.*
5. *Then add fresh basil, salt, tomato, and grated cheese.*
6. *Stir well.*
7. *Add heavy cream and cooked penne.*
8. *Cook the meal for 5 minutes more over the medium heat. Stir it from time to time.*

Nutrition: Calories 388 Fat 23.4 Fiber 0.2 Carbs 17.6 Protein 17.6

Light Paprika Moussaka

Preparation Time: 15 minutes

Cooking Time: 45 minutes

Servings: 3

Ingredients:

- *1 eggplant, trimmed*
- *1 cup ground chicken*
- *1/3 cup white onion, diced*
- *3 oz. Cheddar cheese, shredded*
- *1 potato, sliced*
- *1 teaspoon olive oil*
- *1 teaspoon salt*
- *½ cup milk*
- *1 tablespoon butter*

- *1 tablespoon ground paprika*
- *1 tablespoon Italian seasoning*
- *1 teaspoon tomato paste*

Directions:

1. Slice the eggplant lengthwise and sprinkle with salt.
2. Pour olive oil in the skillet and add sliced potato.
3. Roast potato for 2 minutes from each side.
4. Then transfer it in the plate.
5. Put eggplant in the skillet and roast it for 2 minutes from each side too.
6. Pour milk in the pan and bring it to boil.
7. Add tomato paste, Italian seasoning, paprika, butter, and Cheddar cheese.
8. Then mix up together onion with ground chicken.
9. Arrange the sliced potato in the casserole in one layer.
10. Then add ½ part of all sliced eggplants.
11. Spread the eggplants with ½ part of chicken mixture.
12. Then add remaining eggplants.
13. Pour the milk mixture over the eggplants.
14. Bake moussaka for 30 minutes at 355F.

Nutrition: Calories 387, Fat 21.2, Fiber 8.9, Carbs 26.3, Protein 25.4

Cucumber Bowl with Spices and Greek Yogurt

Preparation Time: *10 minutes*

Cooking Time: *20 minutes*

Servings: *3*

Ingredients:

- *4 cucumbers*
- *½ teaspoon chili pepper*
- *¼ cup fresh parsley, chopped*
- *¾ cup fresh dill, chopped*
- *2 tablespoons lemon juice*
- *½ teaspoon salt*
- *½ teaspoon ground black pepper*
- *¼ teaspoon sage*
- *½ teaspoon dried oregano*
- *1/3 cup Greek yogurt*

Directions:

1. *Make the cucumber dressing: blend the dill and parsley until you get green mash.*
2. *Then combine together green mash with lemon juice, salt, ground black pepper, sage, dried oregano, Greek yogurt, and chili pepper.*
3. *Churn the mixture well.*

4. Chop the cucumbers roughly and combine them with cucumber dressing. Mix up well.
5. Refrigerate the cucumber for 20 minutes.

Nutrition: Calories 114 Fat 1.6 Fiber 4.1 Carbs 23.2 Protein 7.6

Stuffed Bell Peppers with Quinoa

Preparation Time: 10 minutes

Cooking Time: 35 minutes

Servings: 2

Ingredients:

- 2 bell peppers
- 1/3 cup quinoa
- 3 oz. chicken stock
- ¼ cup onion, diced
- ½ teaspoon salt
- ¼ teaspoon tomato paste
- ½ teaspoon dried oregano
- 1/3 cup sour cream
- 1 teaspoon paprika

Directions:

1. Trim the bell peppers and remove the seeds.
2. Then combine together chicken stock and quinoa in the pan.

3. *Add salt and boil the ingredients for 10 minutes or until quinoa will soak all liquid.*
4. *Then combine together cooked quinoa with dried oregano, tomato paste, and onion.*
5. *Fill the bell peppers with the quinoa mixture and arrange in the casserole mold.*
6. *Add sour cream and bake the peppers for 25 minutes at 365F.*
7. *Serve the cooked peppers with sour cream sauce from the casserole mold.*

Nutrition: Calories 237 Fat 10.3 Fiber 4.5 Carbs 31.3 Protein 6.9

Mediterranean Burrito

Preparation Time: 10 minutes

Cooking Time: 0 minutes

Servings: 2

Ingredients:

- *2 wheat tortillas*
- *2 oz. red kidney beans, canned, drained*
- *2 tablespoons hummus*
- *2 teaspoons tahini sauce*
- *1 cucumber*
- *2 lettuce leaves*
- *1 tablespoon lime juice*
- *1 teaspoon olive oil*
- *½ teaspoon dried oregano*

Directions:

1. *Mash the red kidney beans until you get a puree.*
2. *Then spread the wheat tortillas with beans mash from one side.*
3. *Add hummus and tahini sauce.*
4. *Cut the cucumber into the wedges and place them over tahini sauce.*
5. *Then add lettuce leaves.*

6. *Make the dressing: mix up together olive oil, dried oregano, and lime juice.*
7. *Drizzle the lettuce leaves with the dressing and wrap the wheat tortillas in the shape of burritos.*

Nutrition: Calories 288 Fat 10.2 Fiber 14.6 Carbs 38.2 Protein 12.5

Sweet Potato Bacon Mash

Preparation Time: 10 minutes

Cooking Time: 20 minutes

Servings: 4

Ingredients:

- 3 sweet potatoes, peeled
- 4 oz. bacon, chopped
- 1 cup chicken stock
- 1 tablespoon butter
- 1 teaspoon salt
- 2 oz. Parmesan, grated

Directions:

1. Chop sweet potato and put it in the pan.
2. Add chicken stock and close the lid.
3. Boil the vegetables for 15 minutes or until they are soft.
4. After this, drain the chicken stock.
5. Mash the sweet potato with the help of the potato masher. Add grated cheese and butter.
6. Mix up together salt and chopped bacon. Fry the mixture until it is crunchy (10-15 minutes).
7. Add cooked bacon in the mashed sweet potato and mix up with the help of the spoon.
8. It is recommended to serve the meal warm or hot.

Nutrition: Calories 304 Fat 18.1 Fiber 2.9 Carbs 18.8 Protein 17

Prosciutto Wrapped Mozzarella Balls

Preparation Time: 10 minutes

Cooking Time: 10 minutes

Servings: 4

Ingredients:

- *8 Mozzarella balls, cherry size*
- *4 oz. bacon, sliced*
- *¼ teaspoon ground black pepper*
- *¾ teaspoon dried rosemary*
- *1 teaspoon butter*

Directions:

1. *Sprinkle the sliced bacon with ground black pepper and dried rosemary.*
2. *Wrap every Mozzarella ball in the sliced bacon and secure them with toothpicks.*
3. *Melt butter.*
4. *Brush wrapped Mozzarella balls with butter.*
5. *Line the tray with the baking paper and arrange Mozzarella balls in it.*
6. *Bake the meal for 10 minutes at 365F.*

Nutrition: Calories 323 Fat 26.8 Fiber 0.1 Carbs 0.6 Protein 20.6

Garlic Chicken Balls

Preparation Time: 15 minutes

Cooking Time: 10 minutes

Servings: 4

Ingredients:

- 2 cups ground chicken
- 1 teaspoon minced garlic
- 1 teaspoon dried dill
- 1/3 carrot, grated
- 1 egg, beaten
- 1 tablespoon olive oil
- ¼ cup coconut flakes
- ½ teaspoon salt

Directions:

1. In the mixing bowl mix up together ground chicken, minced garlic, dried dill, carrot, egg, and salt.
2. Stir the chicken mixture with the help of the fingertips until homogenous.
3. Then make medium balls from the mixture.
4. Coat every chicken ball in coconut flakes.
5. Heat up olive oil in the skillet.
6. Add chicken balls and cook them for 3 minutes from each side. The cooked chicken balls will have a golden-brown color.

Nutrition: Calories 200 Fat 11.5 Fiber 0.6 Carbs 1.7 Protein 21.9

Air Fryer Asparagus

Preparation Time: 5 minutes

Cooking Time: 8 minutes

Servings: 1

Ingredients:

- *Nutritional yeast*

- *Olive oil non-stick spray*

- *One bunch of asparagus*

Directions:

1. Wash the asparagus. Do not forget to trim off thick, woody ends.

2. Spray with olive oil spray and sprinkle with yeast.

3. In your Instant Crisp Air Fryer, lay the asparagus in a singular layer. Set the temperature to 360°F. Limit the time to eight minutes.

4. *Nutrition: Calories: 17 Fat: 4 g Protein: 9 g*

SALAD RECIPES

Romaine Lettuce and Radicchios Mix

Preparation Time: 6 minutes

Cooking Time: 0 minutes

Servings: 4

Ingredients:

- *2 tablespoons olive oil*
- *A pinch of salt and black pepper*
- *2 spring onions, chopped*
- *3 tablespoons Dijon mustard*
- *Juice of 1 lime*
- *½ cup basil, chopped*
- *4 cups romaine lettuce heads, chopped*
- *3 radicchios, sliced*

Directions:

1. *In a salad bowl, mix the lettuce with the spring onions and the other ingredients, toss and serve.*

Nutrition: Calories: 87, Fats: 2 g, Fiber: 1 g, Carbs: 1 g, Protein: 2 g

Greek Salad

Preparation Time: 15 Minutes

Cooking Time: 15 Minutes

Servings: 5

Ingredients:

For Dressing:

- *½ teaspoon black pepper*
- *¼ teaspoon salt*
- *½ teaspoon oregano*
- *1 tablespoon garlic powder*
- *2 tablespoons Balsamic*
- *1/3 cup olive oil*

For Salad:

- *½ cup sliced black olives*
- *½ cup chopped parsley, fresh*
- *1 small red onion, thin-sliced*
- *1 cup cherry tomatoes, sliced*
- *1 bell pepper, yellow, chunked*
- *1 cucumber, peeled, quarter and slice*
- *4 cups chopped romaine lettuce*
- *½ teaspoon salt*
- *2 tablespoons olive oil*

Directions:

1. *In a small bowl, blend all of the ingredients for the dressing and let this set in the refrigerator while you make the salad.*

2. To assemble the salad, mix together all the ingredients in a large-sized bowl and toss the veggies gently but thoroughly to mix.
3. Serve the salad with the dressing in amounts as desired

Nutrition: Calories: 234, Fat: 16.1 g, Protein: 5 g, Carbs: 48 g

Asparagus and Smoked Salmon Salad

Preparation Time: 15 minutes

Cooking Time: 10 minutes

Servings: 8

Ingredients:

- 1 lb. fresh asparagus, trimmed and cut into 1 inch pieces
- 1/2 cup pecans,
- 2 heads red leaf lettuce, rinsed and torn
- 1/2 cup frozen green peas, thawed
- 1/4 lb. smoked salmon, cut into 1 inch chunks
- 1/4 cup olive oil
- 2 tablespoons. lemon juice
- 1 teaspoon Dijon mustard
- 1/2 teaspoon salt
- 1/4 teaspoon pepper

Directions:

1. *Boil a pot of water. Stir in asparagus and cook for 5 minutes until tender. Let it drain; set aside.*
2. *In a skillet, cook the pecans over medium heat for 5 minutes, stirring constantly until lightly toasted.*
3. *Combine the asparagus, toasted pecans, salmon, peas, and red leaf lettuce and toss in a large bowl.*
4. *In another bowl, combine lemon juice, pepper, Dijon mustard, salt, and olive oil. You can coat the salad with the dressing or serve it on its side.*

Nutrition: Calories: 159 Total Carbohydrate: 7 g Cholesterol: 3 mg Total Fat: 12.9 g Protein: 6 g Sodium: 304 mg

Shrimp Cobb Salad

Preparation Time: 25 minutes

Cooking Time: 10 minutes

Servings: 2

Ingredients:

- *4 slices center-cut bacon*
- *1 lb. large shrimp, peeled and deveined*
- *1/2 teaspoon ground paprika*
- *1/4 teaspoon ground black pepper*
- *1/4 teaspoon salt, divided*
- *2 1/2 tablespoons. Fresh lemon juice*
- *1 1/2 tablespoons. Extra-virgin olive oil*
- *1/2 teaspoon whole grain Dijon mustard*

- 1 (10 oz.) package romaine lettuce hearts, chopped
- 2 cups cherry tomatoes, quartered
- 1 ripe avocado, cut into wedges
- 1 cup shredded carrots

Directions:

1. In a large skillet over medium heat, cook the bacon for 4 minutes on each side till crispy.
2. Take away from the skillet and place on paper towels; let cool for 5 minutes. Break the bacon into bits. Pour out most of the bacon fat, leaving behind only 1 tablespoon. in the skillet. Bring the skillet back to medium-high heat. Add black pepper and paprika to the shrimp for seasoning. Cook the shrimp around 2 minutes each side until it is opaque. Sprinkle with 1/8 teaspoon of salt for seasoning.
3. Combine the remaining 1/8 teaspoon of salt, mustard, olive oil and lemon juice together in a small bowl. Stir in the romaine hearts.
4. On each serving plate, place on 1 and 1/2 cups of romaine lettuce. Add on top the same amounts of avocado, carrots, tomatoes, shrimp and bacon.

Nutrition: Calories: 528 Total Carbohydrate: 22.7 g Cholesterol: 365 mg Total Fat: 28.7 g Protein: 48.9 g Sodium: 1166 mg

Toast with Smoked Salmon, Herbed Cream Cheese, and Greens

Preparation Time: *10 minutes*

Cooking Time: *5 minutes*

Servings: *2*

Ingredients:

For the herbed cream cheese:

- ¼ cup cream cheese, at room temperature
- 2 tablespoons chopped fresh flat-leaf parsley
- 2 tablespoons chopped fresh chives or sliced scallion
- ½ teaspoon garlic powder
- ¼ teaspoon kosher salt

For the toast:

- 2 slices bread
- 4 ounces smoked salmon
- Small handful microgreens or sprouts
- 1 tablespoon capers, drained and rinsed
- ¼ small red onion, very thinly sliced

Directions:

1. To make the herbed cream cheese
2. In a medium bowl, combine the cream cheese, parsley, chives, garlic powder, and salt. Using a fork, mix until combined. Chill until ready to use.

3. To make the toast
4. Toast the bread until golden. Spread the herbed cream cheese over each piece of toast, then top with the smoked salmon.
5. Garnish with the microgreens, capers, and red onion.

Nutrition: Calories: 194; Total fat: 8g; Cholesterol: 26mg; Fiber: 2g; Protein: 12g; Sodium: 227mg

Crab Melt with Avocado and Egg

Preparation Time: 15 minutes

Cooking Time: 15 minutes

Servings: 2

Ingredients:

- 2 English muffins, split
- 3 tablespoons butter, divided
- 2 tomatoes, cut into slices
- 1 (4-ounce) can lump crabmeat
- 6 ounces sliced or shredded cheddar cheese
- 4 large eggs
- Kosher salt
- 2 large avocados, halved, pitted, and cut into slices
- Microgreens, for garnish

Directions:

1. Preheat the broiler.

2. *Toast the English muffin halves. Place the toasted halves, cut-side up, on a baking sheet.*

3. *Spread 1½ teaspoons of butter evenly over each half, allowing the butter to melt into the crevices. Top each with tomato slices, then divide the crab over each, and finish with the cheese.*

4. *Broil for about 4 minutes until the cheese melts.*

5. *Meanwhile, in a medium skillet over medium heat, melt the remaining 1 tablespoon of butter, swirling to coat the bottom of the skillet. Crack the eggs into the skillet, giving ample space for each. Sprinkle with salt. Cook for about 3 minutes. Flip the eggs and cook the other side until the yolks are set to your liking. Place 1 egg on each English muffin half.*

6. *Top with avocado slices and microgreens.*

Nutrition: Calories: 1221; Total fat: 84g; Cholesterol: 94mg; Fiber: 2g; Protein: 12g; Sodium: 888mg

BEANS AND GRAINS

Barley Risotto

Preparation Time: 15 Minutes

Cooking Time: 7 To 8 Hours

Servings: 8

Ingredients:

- 2¼ cups hulled barley, rinsed
- 1 onion, finely chopped
- 4 garlic cloves, minced
- 1 (8-ounce) package button mushrooms, chopped
- 6 cups low-sodium vegetable broth
- ½ teaspoon dried marjoram leaves
- 1/8 teaspoon freshly ground black pepper
- 2/3 cup grated Parmesan cheese

Directions:

1. In a 6-quart slow cooker, mix the barley, onion, garlic, mushrooms, broth, marjoram, and pepper. Cover and cook on low for 7 to 8 hours, or until the barley has absorbed most of the liquid and is tender, and the vegetables are tender.
2. Stir in the Parmesan cheese and serve.

Nutrition: Calories: 288 Carbohydrates: 45g Sugar: 2g Fiber: 9g Fat: 6g Saturated Fat: 3g Protein: 13g Sodium: 495mg

Risotto With Green Beans, Sweet Potatoes, And Peas

Preparation Time: 20 Minutes

Cooking Time: 4 To 5 Hours

Servings: 8

Ingredients:

- 1 large sweet potato, peeled and chopped
- 1 onion, chopped
- 5 garlic cloves, minced
- 2 cups short-grain brown rice
- 1 teaspoon dried thyme leaves
- 7 cups low-sodium vegetable broth
- 2 cups green beans, cut in half crosswise
- 2 cups frozen baby peas
- 3 tablespoons unsalted butter
- ½ cup grated Parmesan cheese

Directions:

1. In a 6-quart slow cooker, mix the sweet potato, onion, garlic, rice, thyme, and broth. Cover and cook on low for 3 to 4 hours, or until the rice is tender.
2. Stir in the green beans and frozen peas. Cover and cook on low for 30 to 40 minutes or until the vegetables are tender.
3. Stir in the butter and cheese. Cover and cook on low for 20 minutes, then stir and serve.

Nutrition: Calories: 385 Carbohydrates: 52g Sugar: 4g Fiber: 6g Fat: 10g Saturated Fat: 5g Protein: 10g Sodium: 426mg

VEGETABLE RECIPES

Famous Fried Pickles

Preparation Time: 5 minutes

Cooking Time: 15 minutes

Servings: 6

Ingredients:

- 1/3 cup milk
- 1 teaspoon garlic powder
- 2 medium-sized eggs
- 1 teaspoon fine sea salt
- 1/3 teaspoon chili powder
- 1/3 cup all-purpose flour
- 1/2 teaspoon shallot powder
- 2 jars sweet and sour pickle spears

Directions:

1. Pat the pickle spears dry with a kitchen towel. Then, take two mixing bowls.
2. Whisk the egg and milk in a bowl. In another bowl, combine all dry ingredients.
3. Firstly, dip the pickle spears into the dry mix; then coat each pickle with the egg/milk mixture; dredge them in the flour mixture again for additional coating.
4. Air fry battered pickles for 15 minutes at 385 degrees. Enjoy!

Nutrition: Calories: 58 Fat: 2g Carbs: 6.8g Protein: 3.2g Sugars: 0.9g Fiber: 0.4g

Fried Squash Croquettes

Preparation Time: 5 minutes

Cooking Time: 17 minutes

Servings: 4

Ingredients:

- *1/3 cup all-purpose flour*
- *1/3 teaspoon freshly ground black pepper, or more to taste*
- *1/3 teaspoon dried sage*
- *4 cloves garlic, minced*
- *1 ½ tablespoons olive oil*
- *1/3 butternut squash, peeled and grated*
- *2 eggs, well whisked*
- *1 teaspoon fine sea salt*
- *A pinch of ground allspice*

Directions:

1. *Thoroughly combine all ingredients in a mixing bowl.*
2. *Preheat your Air Fryer to 345 degrees and set the timer for 17 minutes; cook until your fritters are browned; serve right away.*

Nutrition: Calories: 152 Fat: 10.02g Carbs: 9.4g Protein: 5.8g Sugars: 0.3g Fiber: 0.4g

Tamarind Glazed Sweet Potatoes

Preparation Time: 2 minutes

Cooking Time: 22 minutes

Servings: 4

Ingredients:

- *1/3 teaspoon white pepper*
- *1 tablespoon butter, melted*
- *1/2 teaspoon turmeric powder*
- *5 garnet sweet potatoes, peeled and diced*
- *A few drops liquid Stevia*
- *2 teaspoons tamarind paste*
- *1 1/2 tablespoons fresh lime juice*
- *1 1/2 teaspoon ground allspice*

Directions:

1. *In a mixing bowl, toss all ingredients until sweet potatoes are well coated.*
2. *Air-fry them at 335 degrees F for 12 minutes.*
3. *Pause the Air Fryer and toss again. Increase the temperature to 390 degrees F and cook for an additional 10 minutes. Eat warm.*

Nutrition: Calories: 103 Fat: 9.1g Carbs: 4.9g Protein: 1.9g Sugars: 1.2g Fiber: 0.3g

Cauliflower Crust Pizza

Preparation Time: 20 minutes

Cooking Time: 45 minutes

Servings: 4

Ingredients:

- *1 cauliflower (it should be cut into smaller portions)*

- *1/4 grated parmesan cheese*

- *1 egg*

- *1 tsp. Italian seasoning*

- *1/4 tsp. kosher salt*

- *2 cups of freshly grated mozzarella*

- *1/4 cup of spicy pizza sauce*

- *Basil leaves, for garnishing*

Directions:

1. *Begin by preheating your oven while using the parchment paper to rim the baking sheet.*

2. *Process the cauliflower into a fine powder, and then transfer to a bowl before putting it into the microwave.*

3. *Leave for about 5-6 minutes to get it soft.*

4. *Transfer the microwaved cauliflower to a clean and dry kitchen towel.*

5. *Leave it to cool off.*

6. *When cold, use the kitchen towel to wrap the cauliflower and then get rid of all the moisture by wringing the towel.*

7. *Continue squeezing until water is gone completely.*

8. *Put the cauliflower, Italian seasoning, Parmesan, egg, salt, and mozzarella (1 cup).*

9. *Stir very well until well combined.*

10. *Transfer the combined mixture to the baking sheet previously prepared, pressing it into a 10-inch round shape.*

11. *Bake for 10-15 minutes until it becomes golden in color.*

12. *Take the baked crust out of the oven and use the spicy pizza sauce and mozzarella (the leftover 1 cup) to top it.*

13. *Bake again for 10 more minutes until the cheese melts and looks bubbly.*

14. *Garnish using fresh basil leaves.*

15. *You can also enjoy this with salad.*

Nutrition: Calories: 74 Cal Carbohydrates: 4 g Protein: 6 g Fat: 4 g Fiber: 2 g

Roasted Squash Puree

Preparation Time: 20 minutes

Cooking Time: 6 to 7 hours

Servings: 8

Ingredients:

- *1 (3-pound) butternut squash, peeled, seeded, and cut into 1-inch pieces*

- *3 (1-pound) acorn squash, peeled, seeded, and cut into 1-inch pieces*

- *2 onions, chopped*

- *3 garlic cloves, minced*

- *2 tablespoons olive oil*

- *1 teaspoon dried marjoram leaves*

- *1/2 teaspoon salt*

- *1/8 teaspoon freshly ground black pepper*

Directions:

1. *In a 6-quart slow cooker, mix all of the ingredients.*

2. Cover and cook on low for 6 to 7 hours, or until the squash is tender when pierced with a fork.

3. Use a potato masher to mash the squash right in the slow cooker.

Nutrition: Calories: 175 Cal Carbohydrates: 38 g Sugar: 1 g Fiber: 3 g Fat: 4 g Saturated Fat: 1 g Protein: 3 g Sodium: 149 mg

Creamy Spinach and Mushroom Lasagna

Preparation Time: 60 minutes

Cooking Time: 20 minutes

Servings: 6

Ingredients:

- 10 lasagna noodles

- 1 package whole milk ricotta

- 2 packages of frozen chopped spinach.

- 4 cups mozzarella cheese (divided and shredded)

- 3/4 cup grated fresh Parmesan

- 3 tablespoons chopped fresh parsley leaves (optional)

For the Sauce:

- 1/4 cup of butter (unsalted)

- *2 cloves garlic*

- *1 pound of thinly sliced cremini mushroom*

- *1 diced onion*

- *1/4 cup flour*

- *4 cups milk, kept at room temperature*

- *1 teaspoon basil (dried)*

- *Pinch of nutmeg*

- *Salt and freshly ground black pepper, to taste*

Directions:

1. *Preheat oven to 352 degrees F.*

2. *To make the sauce, over a medium heat, melt your butter. Add garlic, mushrooms, and onion. Cook and stir at intervals until it becomes tender at about 3-4 minutes.*

3. *Whisk in flour until lightly browned, it takes about 1 minute for it to become brown.*

4. *Next, whisk in the milk gradually, and cook, constantly whisking, about 2-3 minutes till it becomes thickened. Stir in basil, oregano, and nutmeg, season with salt and pepper for taste.*

5. *Then set aside.*

6. In another pot of boiling salted water, cook lasagna noodles according to the package instructions.

7. Spread one cup mushroom sauce onto the bottom of a baking dish; top it with four lasagna noodles, 1/2 of the spinach, one cup mozzarella cheese, and 1/4 cup Parmesan.

8. Repeat this process with remaining noodles, mushroom sauce, and cheeses.

9. Place into oven and bake for 35-45 minutes, or until it starts bubbling. Then boil for 2-3 minutes until it becomes brown and translucent.

10. Let cool for 15 minutes.

11. Serve it with garnished parsley (optional)

Nutrition: Calories: 488.3 Cal Fats: 19.3 g Cholesterol: 88.4 mg Sodium: 451.9 mg Carbohydrates: 51.0 g Dietary Fiber: 7.0 g Protein: 25.0 g

Thai Roasted Veggies

Preparation Time: 20 minutes

Cooking Time: 6 to 8 hours

Servings: 8

Ingredients:

- 4 large carrots, peeled and cut into chunks

- *2 onions, peeled and sliced*

- *6 garlic cloves, peeled and sliced*

- *2 parsnips, peeled and sliced*

- *2 jalapeño peppers, minced*

- *1/2 cup Roasted Vegetable Broth*

- *1/3 cup canned coconut milk*

- *3 tablespoons lime juice*

- *2 tablespoons grated fresh ginger root*

- *2 teaspoons curry powder*

Directions:

1. *In a 6-quart slow cooker, mix the carrots, onions, garlic, parsnips, and jalapeño peppers.*

2. *In a small bowl, mix the vegetable broth, coconut milk, lime juice, ginger root, and curry powder until well blended. Pour this mixture into the slow cooker.*

3. *Cover and cook on low for 6 to 8 hours, do it until the vegetables are tender when pierced with a fork.*

Nutrition: Calories: 69 Cal Carbohydrates: 13 g Sugar: 6 g Fiber: 3 g Fat: 3g Saturated Fat: 3g Protein: 1g Sodium: 95mg

Crispy-Topped Baked Vegetables

Preparation Time: 10 minutes

Cooking Time: 40 minutes

Servings: 4

Ingredients:

- 2 tbsp. olive oil
- 1 onion, chopped
- 1 celery stalk, chopped
- 2 carrots, grated
- 1/2-pound turnips, sliced
- 1 cup vegetable broth
- 1 tsp. turmeric
- Sea salt and black pepper, to taste
- 1/2 tsp. liquid smoke
- 1 cup Parmesan cheese, shredded
- 2 tbsp fresh chives, chopped

Directions:

1. *Set oven to 360°F and grease a baking dish with olive oil.*

2. *Set a skillet over medium heat and warm olive oil.*

3. *Sweat the onion until soft, and place in the turnips, carrots, and celery; and cook for 4 minutes.*

4. *Remove the vegetable mixture to the baking dish.*

5. *Combine vegetable broth with turmeric, pepper, liquid smoke, and salt.*

6. *Spread this mixture over the vegetables.*

7. *Sprinkle with Parmesan cheese and bake for about 30 minutes.*

8. *Garnish with chives to serve.*

Nutrition: Calories: 242 Cal Fats: 16.3 g Carbohydrates: 8.6 g Protein: 16.3 g

Roasted Root Vegetables

Preparation Time: 20 minutes

Cooking Time: 6 to 8 hours

Servings: 8

Ingredients:

- *6 carrots, cut into 1-inch chunks*

- *2 yellow onions, each cut into 8 wedges*

- *2 sweet potatoes, peeled and cut into chunks*

- *6 Yukon Gold potatoes, cut into chunks*

- *8 whole garlic cloves, peeled*

- *4 parsnips, peeled and cut into chunks*

- *3 tablespoons olive oil*

- *1 teaspoon dried thyme leaves*

- *1/2 teaspoon salt*

- *1/8 teaspoon freshly ground black pepper*

Directions:

1. *In a 6-quart slow cooker, mix all of the ingredients.*

2. *Cover and cook on low for 6 to 8 hours, or until the vegetables are tender.*

3. *Serve and enjoy!*

Nutrition: Calories: 214 Cal Carbohydrates: 40 g Sugar: 7 g Fiber: 6 g Fat: 5 g Saturated Fat: 1 g Protein: 4 g Sodium: 201 mg

HUMMUS

Preparation Time: 10 minutes

Cooking Time: 10 minutes

Servings: 32

Ingredients:

- 4 cups of cooked garbanzo beans

- 1 cup of water

- 1 1/2 tablespoons of lemon juice

- 2 teaspoons of ground cumin

- 1 1/2 teaspoon of ground coriander.

- 1 teaspoon of finely chopped garlic

- 1/2 teaspoon of salt

- 1/4 teaspoon of fresh ground pepper

- Paprika for garnish

Directions:

1. On a food processor, place together the garbanzo beans, lemon juice, water, garlic, salt, and pepper and process it until it becomes smooth and creamy.

2. To achieve your desired consistency, add more water.

3. *Then spoon out the hummus in a serving bowl*

4. *Sprinkle your paprika and serve.*

Nutrition: Protein: 0.7 g Carbohydrates: 2.5 g Dietary Fiber: 0.6 g Sugars: 0 g Fat: 1.7 g

Vegan Edamame Quinoa Collard Wraps

Preparation Time: 5 minutes

Cooking Time: 15 minutes

Servings: 4

Ingredients:

For the wrap:

- *Collard leaves; 2 to 3*

- *Grated carrot; 1/4 cup*

- *Sliced cucumber; 1/4 cup*

- *Red bell pepper; 1/4; thin strips*

- *Orange bell pepper; 1/4; thin strips*

- *Cooked quinoa; 1/3 cup*

- *Shelled defrosted edamame; 1/3 cup*

For the dressing:

- *Fresh ginger root; 3 tablespoons; peeled and chopped*

- *Cooked chickpeas; 1 cup*

- *Clove of garlic; 1*

- *Rice vinegar; 4 tablespoons*

- *Low sodium tamari/coconut aminos; 2 tablespoons*

- *Lime juice; 2 tablespoons*

- *Water; 1/4 cup*

- *Few pinches of chili flakes*

- *Stevia; 1 pack*

Directions:

1. *For the dressing, combine all the ingredients and purée in a food processor until smooth.*

2. *Load into a little jar or tub, and set aside.*

3. *Place the collar leaves on a flat surface, covering one another to create a tighter tie.*

4. *Take one tablespoon of ginger dressing and blend it up with the prepared quinoa.*

5. *Spoon the prepared quinoa onto the leaves and shape a simple horizontal line at the closest end.*

6. *Supplement the edamame with all the veggie fillings left over.*

7. *Drizzle around one tablespoon of the ginger dressing on top, then fold the cover's sides inwards.*

8. *Pullover the fillings, the side of the cover closest to you, then turn the whole body away to seal it up.*

Nutrition: Calories: 295 Cal Sugar: 3 g Sodium: 200 mg Fat: 13 g

SAUCES, SOUP AND STEW RECIPES

Coconut and Shrimp Bisque

Preparation Time: 10 minutes

Cooking Time: 15 minutes

Servings: 4

Ingredients:

- ¼ cup red curry paste
- 2 tablespoons water
- 1 tablespoon extra-virgin olive oil
- 1 bunch scallions, sliced
- 1-pound medium (21-30 count) shrimp, peeled and deveined
- 1 cup frozen peas
- 1 red bell pepper, diced
- 1 (14-ounce) can full-fat coconut milk
- Kosher salt

Directions:

1. In a small bowl, whisk together the red curry paste and water. Set aside.
2. Select sear/sauté and set to med. Select start/stop to begin. Let preheat for 3 minutes.
3. Add the oil and scallions. Cook for 2 minutes.

4. *Add the shrimp, peas, and bell pepper. Stir well to combine. Stir in the red curry paste. Cook for 5 minutes, until the peas are tender.*

5. *Stir in coconut milk and cook for an additional 5 minutes until shrimp is cooked through and the bisque is thoroughly heated.*

6. *Season with salt and serve immediately.*

Nutrition: Calories: 460 Total Fat: 32g Saturated Fat: 23g Cholesterol: 223mg Sodium: 902mg Carbohydrates: 16g Fiber: 5g Protein: 29g

Roasted Tomato and Seafood Stew

Preparation Time: 10 minutes

Cooking Time: 46 minutes

Servings: 6

Ingredients:

- *2 tablespoons extra-virgin olive oil*
- *1 yellow onion, diced*
- *1 fennel bulb, tops removed and bulb diced*
- *3 garlic cloves, minced*
- *1 cup dry white wine*
- *2 (14.5-ounce) cans fire-roasted tomatoes*
- *2 cups chicken stock*
- *1-pound medium (21-30 count) shrimp, peeled and deveined*
- *1-pound raw white fish (cod or haddock), cubed*
- *Salt*
- *Freshly ground black pepper*
- *Fresh basil, torn, for garnish*

Directions:

1. *Select sear/sauté and set to med. Select start/stop to begin. Let preheat for 3 minutes.*
2. *Add the olive oil, onions, fennel, and garlic. Cook for about 3 minutes, until translucent.*

3. *Add the white wine and deglaze, scraping any stuck bits from the bottom of the pot using a silicone spatula. Add the roasted tomatoes and chicken stock. Simmer for 25 to 30 minutes. Add the shrimp and white fish.*

4. *Select sear/sauté and set to md: lo. Select start/stop to begin.*

5. *Simmer for 10 minutes, stirring frequently, until the shrimp and fish are cooked through. Season with salt and pepper.*

6. *Ladle into bowl and serve topped with torn basil.*

Nutrition: Calories: 301 Total fat: 8g Saturated Fat: 1g Cholesterol: 99mg Sodium: 808mg Carbohydrates: 21g Fiber: 4g Protein: 26g

Chicken Potpie Soup

Preparation Time: 15 minutes

Cooking Time: 1 hour

Servings: 6

Ingredients:

- 4 (8-ounce) chicken breasts
- 2 cups chicken stock
- 2 tablespoons unsalted butter
- 1 yellow onion, diced
- 16 ounces frozen mixed vegetables
- 1 cup heavy (whipping) cream
- 1 (10.5-ounce) can condensed cream of chicken soup
- 2 tablespoons cornstarch
- 2 tablespoons water
- Salt
- Freshly ground black pepper
- 1 (16.3-ounce) tube refrigerated biscuit dough

Directions:

1. Place the chicken and stock in the pot. Assemble pressure lid, making sure the pressure release valve is in the seal position.
2. Select pressure and set to hi. Set time to 15 minutes. Select start/stop to begin.

3. *Once pressure cooking is complete, quick release the pressure by turning the pressure release valve to the vent position. Carefully remove lid when the unit has finished releasing pressure.*

4. *Using a silicone-tipped utensil, shred the chicken.*

5. *Select sear/sauté and set to med. Add the butter, onion, mixed vegetables, cream, and condensed soup and stir. Select start/stop to begin. Simmer for 10 minutes.*

6. *In a small bowl, whisk together the cornstarch and water. Slowly whisk the cornstarch mixture into the soup. Set temperature to low and simmer for 10 minutes more. Season with salt and pepper.*

7. *Carefully arrange the biscuits on top of the simmering soup. Close crisping lid.*

8. *Select bake/roast, set temperature to 325°f, and set time to 15 minutes. Select start/stop to begin.*

9. *When cooking is complete, remove the biscuits. To serve, place a biscuit in a bowl and ladle soup over it.*

Nutrition: Calories: 731 Total Fat: 26g Saturated Fat: 17g Cholesterol: 169mg Sodium: 1167mg Carbohydrates: 56g Fiber: 5g Protein: 45g

Tex-Mex Chicken Tortilla Soup

Preparation Time: 10 minutes

Cooking Time: 20 minutes

Servings: 8

Ingredients:

- 1 tablespoon extra-virgin olive oil
- 1 onion, chopped
- 1 pound boneless, skinless chicken breasts
- 6 cups chicken broth
- 1 (12-ounce) jar salsa
- 4 ounces' tomato paste
- 1 tablespoon chili powder
- 2 teaspoons cumin
- ½ teaspoon sea salt
- ½ teaspoon freshly ground black pepper
- 1 pinch of cayenne pepper
- 1 (15-ounce) can black beans, rinsed and drained
- 2 cups frozen corn
- Tortilla strips, for garnish

Directions:

1. Select sear/sauté and set to temperature to hi. Select start/stop to begin. Let preheat for 5 minutes.

2. *Place the olive oil and onions into the pot and cook, stirring occasionally, for 5 minutes.*

3. *Add the chicken breast, chicken broth, salsa, tomato paste, chili powder, cumin, salt, pepper, and cayenne pepper. Assemble pressure lid, making sure the pressure release valve is in the seal position.*

4. *When pressure cooking is complete, allow pressure to release naturally for 10 minutes. After 10 minutes, quickly relieve residual pressure by moving the pressure relief valve to the vent position. Carefully remove the cover when the unit has finished releasing pressure.*

5. *Transfer the chicken breasts to a cutting board and shred with two forks. Set aside.*

6. *Add the black beans and corn. Select sear/sauté and set to md. Select start/stop to begin. Cook until heated through, about 5 minutes.*

7. *Add shredded chicken back to the pot. Garnish with tortilla strips, serve, and enjoy!*

Nutrition: Calories: 186 Total Fat: 4g Saturated Fat: 0g Cholesterol: 33mg Sodium: 783mg Carbohydrates: 23g Fiber: 6g Protein: 19g

Homemade Chicken Broth

Preparation Time: 5 minutes

Cooking Time: 30 minutes

Servings: 4

Ingredients:

- *1 tablespoon olive oil*
- *1 chopped onion*
- *2 chopped stalks celery*
- *2 chopped carrots*
- *1 whole chicken*
- *2+ quarts of water*
- *1 tablespoon salt*
- *½ teaspoon pepper*
- *1 teaspoon fresh sage*

Directions:

1. *Sauté vegetables in oil.*
2. *Add chicken and water and simmer for 2+ hours until the chicken falls off the bone. Keep adding water as needed.*
3. *Remove the chicken carcass from the broth, place on a platter, and let it cool. Pull chicken off the carcass and put it into the broth.*

4. *Pour broth mixture into pint and quart mason jars. Be sure to add meat to each jar.*
5. *Leave one full inch of space from the top of the jar or it will crack when it freezes as liquids expand. Place jars in freezer for up to a year.*
6. *Take out and use whenever you make a soup.*

Nutrition: Calories: 213 Fat: 6g Fiber: 13g Carbs: 16g Protein: 22g

Homemade Vegetable Broth

Preparation Time: 5 minutes

Cooking Time: 30 minutes

Servings: 4

Ingredients:

- *1 tablespoon olive oil*
- *1 chopped onion*
- *2 chopped stalks celery*
- *2 chopped carrots*
- *1 head bok choy*
- *6 cups or 1 package fresh spinach*
- *2+ quarts of water*
- *1 tablespoon salt*
- *½ teaspoon pepper*
- *1 teaspoon fresh sage*

Directions:

1. *Sauté vegetables in oil. Add water and simmer for 1 hour.*
2. *Keep adding water as needed.*
3. *Pour broth mixture into pint and quart mason jars.*
4. *Leave one full inch of space from the top of the jar or it will crack when it freezes as liquids expand. Place jars in freezer for up to a year.*

5. *Take out and use whenever you make a soup.*

Nutrition: *Calories: 140 Fat: 2g Fiber: 23g Carbs: 22g Protein: 47g*

Fish Stew

Preparation Time: *5 minutes*

Cooking Time: *30 minutes*

Servings: *4*

Ingredients:

- *1 tablespoon olive oil*
- *1 chopped onion or leek*
- *2 chopped stalks celery*
- *2 chopped carrots*
- *1 clove minced garlic*
- *1 tablespoon parsley*
- *1 bay leaf*
- *1 clove*
- *1/8 teaspoon kelp or dulse (seaweed)*
- *¼ teaspoon salt*
- *Fish—leftover, cooked, diced*
- *2–3 cups chicken or vegetable broth*

Directions:

1. *Add all of ingredients and simmer on the stove for 20 minutes.*

Nutrition: Calories: 342 Fat: 15g Fiber: 11g Carbs: 8gProtein: 10g

Black Bean Soup

Preparation Time: 5 minutes

Cooking Time: 1 hour

Servings: 4

Ingredients:

- *1 pound dry black beans (soak in water overnight and drain water)*
- *1 tablespoon olive oil*
- *2 cups chopped onion or 1 leek*
- *1 cup chopped carrots*
- *4 cloves minced garlic*
- *2 teaspoons cumin*
- *¼ teaspoon red pepper flakes*
- *4 cups chicken broth*
- *4 cups water*
- *¼ teaspoon thyme*
- *2 chopped tomatoes or 1 (14 oz) can tomatoes*
- *1½ teaspoon salt*
- *Optional: add bacon or ham to flavor*
- *Chopped green onions to garnish*

Directions:

1. Sauté vegetables in oil. Add rest of ingredients and cook on stovetop on medium-low heat for 1 hour.

Nutrition: Calories: 508 Fat: 12g Fiber: 9g Carbs: 24gProtein: 40g

Richard's Best Chicken

Preparation Time: 5 minutes

Cooking Time: 30 minutes

Servings: 4

Ingredients:

- *2 tablespoons olive oil*
- *8 chicken thighs*
- *6 cloves garlic*
- *1 jar artichoke hearts, drained*
- *¾ cup chicken broth*
- *3 fresh squeezed oranges*
- *1 sliced Meyer lemon*
- *¼ cup capers*
- *½ cup olives*

Directions:

1. *In a cast-iron skillet, fry chicken on each side in oil until skin is golden and crispy. Remove from skillet.*
2. *Sauté garlic and artichokes for a few minutes, add chicken (skin up). Pour in rest of ingredients and bring to a boil.*
3. *Place skillet with all ingredients uncovered in a 350-degree oven for 30 minutes.*

Nutrition: Calories: 285 Fat: 28g Fiber: 7g Carbs: 34g Protein: 23g

White Bean and Cabbage Soup

Preparation Time: 5 minutes

Cooking Time: 30 minutes

Servings: 4

Ingredients:

- *1 tablespoon olive oil*
- *4 chopped carrots*
- *4 chopped stalks of celery or 1 chopped bok choy*
- *1 chopped onion*
- *2 cloves minced garlic*
- *1 chopped cabbage head*
- *½ lb northern beans soaked in water overnight (drained)*
- *6 cups chicken broth*
- *3 cups water*

Directions:

1. *Sauté vegetables in oil.*
2. *Add rest of ingredients and cook on medium-low heat for 30 minutes.*

Nutrition: Calories: 423 Fat: 2g Fiber: 0g Carbs: 20g Protein: 33g

Brooke's Chili

Preparation Time: 5 minutes

Cooking Time: 1 hour

Servings: 4

Ingredients:

- 2 lb organic ground beef
- 1 diced onion
- 3 cloves minced garlic
- 6 diced tomatoes
- 1 jar tomato sauce
- 1 tablespoon salt
- 1 cup water
- 1 cup kidney beans soaked in water overnight (drained)
- 1 cup pinto beans soaked in water overnight (drained)
- 2 tablespoons chili powder
- 1 tablespoon cumin
- 1 tablespoon honey or maple syrup
- 1 teaspoon baking stevia
- 1 teaspoon pepper

Directions:

1. In a large pot, brown the ground beef and drain the grease.
2. Add the onion and garlic and cook until translucent.

3. *Add rest of ingredients and simmer for 1 hour.*

Nutrition: Calories: 110 Fat: 31g Fiber: 18g Carbs: 15g Protein: 12g

LEAN AND GREEN RECIPES

Tomatillo and Green Chili Pork Stew

Preparation Time: 10 minutes

Cooking Time: 20 minutes

Servings: 4

Ingredients:

- 2 scallions, chopped

- 2 cloves of garlic

- 1 lb. tomatillos, trimmed and chopped

- 8 large romaine or green lettuce leaves, divided

- 2 serrano chilies, seeds, and membranes

- ½ tsp of dried Mexican oregano (or you can use regular oregano)

- 1 ½ lb. of boneless pork loin, to be cut into bite-sized cubes

- ¼ cup of cilantro, chopped

- ¼ tablespoon (each) salt and paper

- *1 jalapeno, seeds and membranes to be removed and thinly sliced*

- *1 cup of sliced radishes*

- *4 lime wedges*

Directions:

1. *Combine scallions, garlic, tomatillos, 4 lettuce leaves, serrano chilies, and oregano in a blender. Then puree until smooth*

2. *Put pork and tomatillo mixture in a medium pot. 1-inch of puree should cover the pork; if not, add water until it covers it. Season with pepper & salt, and cover it simmers. Simmer on heat for approximately 20 minutes.*

3. *Now, finely shred the remaining lettuce leaves.*

4. *When the stew is done cooking, garnish with cilantro, radishes, finely shredded lettuce, sliced jalapenos, and lime wedges.*

Nutrition: Calories: 370 Protein: 36g Carbohydrate: 14g Fat: 19 g

Cloud Bread

Preparation Time: 25 minutes

Cooking Time: 35 minutes

Servings: 3

Ingredients:

- *½ cup of Fat-free 0% Plain Greek Yogurt (4.4 0z)*

- *3 Eggs, Separated*

- *16 teaspoon Cream of Tartar*

- *1 Packet sweetener (a granulated sweetener just like stevia)*

Directions:

1. *For about 30 minutes before making this meal, place the Kitchen Aid Bowl and the whisk attachment in the freezer.*

2. *Preheat your oven to 30 degrees*

3. *Remove the mixing bowl and whisk attachment from the freezer*

4. *Separate the eggs. Now put the egg whites in the Kitchen Aid Bowl, and they should be in a different medium-sized bowl.*

5. *In the medium-sized bowl containing the yolks, mix in the sweetener and yogurt.*

6. *In the bowl containing the egg white, add in the cream of tartar. Beat this mixture until the egg whites turn to stiff peaks.*

7. *Now, take the egg yolk mixture and carefully fold it into the egg whites. Be cautious and avoid over-stirring.*

8. *Place baking paper on a baking tray and spray with cooking spray.*

9. *Scoop out 6 equally-sized "blobs" of the "dough" onto the parchment paper.*

10. *Bake for about 25-35 minutes (make sure you check when it is 25 minutes, in some ovens, they are done at this timestamp). You will know they are done as they will get brownish at the top and have some crack.*

11. *Most people like them cold against being warm*

12. *Most people like to re-heat in a toast oven or toaster to get them a little bit crispy.*

13. *Your serving size should be about 2 pieces.*

Nutrition: Calories: 234 Protein: 23g Carbs: 5g Fiber: 8g Sodium: 223g

Avocado Lime Shrimp Salad

Preparation Time: 15 minutes

Cooking Time: 0 minutes

Servings: 2

Ingredients:

- 14 ounces of jumbo cooked shrimp, peeled and deveined; chopped

- 4 ½ ounces of avocado, diced

- 1 ½ cup of tomato, diced

- ¼ cup of chopped green onion

- ¼ cup of jalapeno with the seeds removed, diced fine

- 1 teaspoon of olive oil

- 2 tablespoons of lime juice

- 1/8 teaspoon of salt

- 1 tablespoon of chopped cilantro

Directions:

1. Get a small bowl and combine green onion, olive oil, lime juice, pepper, a pinch of salt. Wait for about 5

minutes for all of them to marinate and mellow the flavor of the onion.

2. *Get a large bowl and combined chopped shrimp, tomato, avocado, jalapeno. Combine all of the ingredients, add cilantro, and gently toss.*

3. *Add pepper and salt as desired.*

Nutrition: Calories: 314 Protein: 26g Carbs: 15g Fiber: 9g

DESSERT RECIPES

Ginger Ice Cream

Preparation Time: 15 minutes

Cooking Time: 10 minutes

Servings: 6

Ingredients:

- 1 mango, peeled
- 1 cup Greek yogurt
- 1 tablespoon Erythritol
- ¼ cup milk
- 1 teaspoon vanilla extract
- ¼ teaspoon ground ginger

Directions:

1. Blend the mango until you get puree and combine it with Erythritol, milk, vanilla extract, and ground ginger.
2. Then mix up together Greek yogurt and mango puree mixture. Transfer it in the plastic vessel.
3. Freeze the ice cream for 35 minutes.

Nutrition: Calories 90, Fat 1.4 g, Fiber 1.4 g, Carbs 21.9 g, Protein 4.9 g

Cherry Compote

Preparation Time: 2 hours

Cooking Time: 0 minutes

Servings: 6

Ingredients:

- 2 peaches, pitted, halved
- 1 cup cherries, pitted
- ½ cup grape juice
- ½ cup strawberries
- 1 tablespoon liquid honey
- 1 teaspoon vanilla extract
- 1 teaspoon ground cinnamon

Directions:

1. Pour grape juice in the saucepan.
2. Add vanilla extract and ground cinnamon. Bring the liquid to boil.
3. After this, put peaches, cherries, and strawberries in the hot grape juice and bring to boil.
4. Remove the mixture from heat, add liquid honey, and close the lid.
5. Let the compote rest for 20 minutes.
6. Carefully mix up the compote and transfer in the serving plate.

Nutrition: Calories 80, Fat 0.4 g, Fiber 2.4 g, Carbs 19.9 g, Protein 0.9 g

Creamy Strawberries

Preparation Time: 15 minutes

Cooking Time: 10 minutes

Servings: 6

Ingredients:

- 6 tablespoons almond butter
- 1 tablespoon Erythritol
- 1 cup milk
- 1 teaspoon vanilla extract
- 1 cup strawberries, sliced

Directions:

1. Pour milk in the saucepan.
2. Add Erythritol, vanilla extract, and almond butter.
3. With the help of the hand mixer mix up the liquid until smooth and bring it to boil.
4. Then remove the mixture from the heat and let it cool.
5. The cooled mixture will be thick.
6. Put the strawberries in the serving glasses and top with the thick almond butter dip.

Nutrition: Calories 192, Fat 14.4 g, Fiber 3.4 g, Carbs 10.9 g, Protein 1.9 g

Chocolate Bars

Preparation Time: *10 minutes*

Cooking Time: *20 minutes*

Servings: *16*

Ingredients:

- *15 oz cream cheese, softened*

- *15 oz unsweetened dark chocolate*

- *1 tsp vanilla*

- *10 drops liquid stevia*

Directions:

1. *Grease 8-inch square dish and set aside.*

2. *In a saucepan dissolve chocolate over low heat.*

3. *Add stevia and vanilla and stir well.*

4. *Remove pan from heat and set aside.*

5. *Add cream cheese into the blender and blend until smooth.*

6. *Add melted chocolate mixture into the cream cheese and blend until just combined.*

7. Transfer mixture into the prepared dish and spread evenly and place in the refrigerator until firm.

8. Slice and serve.

Nutrition: Calories: 230 Fat: 24 g Carbs: 7.5 g Sugar: 0.1 g Protein: 6 g Cholesterol: 29 mg

Blueberry Muffins

Preparation Time: 15 minutes

Cooking Time: 35 minutes

Servings: 12

Ingredients:

- *2 eggs*

- *1/2 cup fresh blueberries*

- *1 cup heavy cream*

- *2 cups almond flour*

- *1/4 tsp lemon zest*

- *1/2 tsp lemon extract*

- *1 tsp baking powder*

- *5 drops stevia*

- *1/4 cup butter, melted*

Directions:

1. *heat the cooker to 350 F. Line muffin tin with cupcake liners and set aside.*

2. *Add eggs into the bowl and whisk until mix.*

3. *Add remaining ingredients and mix to combine.*

4. *Pour mixture into the prepared muffin tin and bake for 25 minutes.*

5. *Serve and enjoy.*

Nutrition: Calories: 190 Fat: 17 g Carbs: 5 g Sugar: 1 g Protein: 5 g Cholesterol: 55 mg

Chia Pudding

Preparation Time: 20 minutes

Cooking Time: 0 minutes

Servings: 2

Ingredients:

- 4 tbsp chia seeds

- 1 cup unsweetened coconut milk

- 1/2 cup raspberries

Directions:

1. Add raspberry and coconut milk into a blender and blend until smooth.

2. Pour mixture into the glass jar.

3. Add chia seeds in a jar and stir well.

4. Seal the jar with a lid and shake well and place in the refrigerator for 3 hours.

5. Serve chilled and enjoy.

Nutrition: Calories: 360 Fat: 33 g Carbs: 13 g Sugar: 5 g Protein: 6 g Cholesterol: 0 mg

30 DAYS MEAL PLAN

Day	Breakfast	Lunch	Dinner
1	Pancakes with berries	Yogurt Garlic Chicken	Zucchini Salmon Salad
2	Omelette à la Margherita	Lemony Parmesan Salmon	Pan Fried Salmon
3	Omelette with tomatoes and spring onions	Easiest Tuna Cobbler Ever	Grilled Salmon with Pineapple Salsa
4	Coconut chia pudding with berries	Deliciously Homemade Pork Buns	Mediterranean Chickpea Salad
5	Eel on scrambled eggs and bread	Mouthwatering Tuna Melts	Warm Chorizo Chickpea Salad
6	Chia seed gel with pomegranate and nuts	Bacon Wings	Greek Roasted Fish
7	Lavender Blueberry Chia Seed Pudding	Pepper Pesto Lamb	Tomato Fish Bake
8	Yogurt with granola and persimmon	Tuna Spinach Casserole	Garlicky Tomato Chicken Casserole
9	Smoothie bowl with spinach, mango and muesli	Greek Style Mini Burger Pies	Chicken Cacciatore
10	Fried egg with bacon	Family Fun Pizza	Fennel Wild Rice Risotto

11	Smoothie bowl with berries, poppy seeds, nuts and seeds	Almond Pancakes	Wild Rice Prawn Salad
12	Whole grain bread and avocado	Mouth-watering Pie	Chicken Broccoli Salad with Avocado Dressing
13	Porridge with walnuts	Chicken Omelet	Seafood Paella
14	Fried egg with bacon	Special Almond Cereal	Herbed Roasted Chicken Breasts
15	Alkaline Blueberry Spelt Pancakes	Awesome Avocado Muffins	Marinated Chicken Breasts
16	Alkaline Blueberry Muffins	Tasty WW Pancakes	Balsamic Beef and Mushrooms Mix
17	Crunchy Quinoa Meal	WW Salad in A Jar	Oregano Pork Mix
18	Coconut Pancakes	WW Breakfast Cereal	Simple Beef Roast
19	Quinoa Porridge	Yummy Smoked Salmon	Chicken Breast Soup
20	Amaranth Porridge	Almond Coconut Cereal	Cauliflower Curry
21	Banana Barley Porridge	Almond Porridge	Pork and Peppers Chili
22	Zucchini Muffins	Asparagus Frittata Recipe	Greek Style Quesadillas

23	Millet Porridge	Avocados Stuffed with Salmon	Creamy Penne
24	Jackfruit Vegetable Fry	Bacon and Brussels Sprout Breakfast	Light Paprika Moussaka
25	Zucchini Pancakes	Bacon and Lemon spiced Muffins	Cucumber Bowl with Spices and Greek Yogurt
26	Squash Hash	Pepper Pesto Lamb	Stuffed Bell Peppers with Quinoa
27	Hemp Seed Porridge	Tropical Greens Smoothie	Mediterranean Burrito
28	Pumpkin Spice Quinoa	Vitamin C Smoothie Cubes	Sweet Potato Bacon Mash
29	Zucchini Muffins	Overnight Chocolate Chia Pudding	Prosciutto Wrapped Mozzarella Balls
30	Tasty Breakfast Donuts	Slow Cooker Savory Butternut Squash Oatmeal	Garlic Chicken Balls

CONCLUSION

Lean and Green can be used effectively for rapid weight loss compared to other plans simply because they supplied lean, green foods and their low calories.

Thanks to the Lean and Green methodology, U.S. News and World Report ranked it number 2 in its ranking of the best quick weight loss diets, however number 32 in its ranking of the best diets for healthy eating. "At the moment, it seems to be inconceivable not to probably lose a few pounds; you're eating a large proportion of the calories that most adults spend," he said. "The viewpoint taken out is less encouraging."

London agrees that there is a unique way to approach lasting weight reduction: "Eating dinners and bites that join piles of products, 100% whole grains, nuts, seeds, vegetables, and heartbeats, low-fat: dairy, eggs, poultry, fish, and lean burgers in addition to certain extravagances is the most ideal approach to get fitter economically for the long haul."

When doing the lean and green diet you should avoid refined grains, sugary drinks, sung food, and alcohol. As you progress and maintain your organization, some carbohydrate-containing foods are incorporated again, for example, low-fat dairy products, and new natural products

However, the diet is costly, repetitive, and doesn't accommodate all nutritional wants. what's more, the extended calorie restriction can also result in nutrient deficiencies and different potential health problems.

Be that as it may, the eating routine is expensive, monotonous, and does not accommodate all nutritional needs. Furthermore, extended calorie restriction may lead to deficiencies in supplements and other potential health problems.

At the same time, since this system promotes weight and fat loss over a rapid period time, research also wants to assess whether it encourages the long-lasting lifestyle adjustments needed.

Some people say that the most challenging part of dieting is the mental effort of figuring out what to eat each day or at each meal.

The lean and green diet alleviates the stress of meal planning and "decision fatigue" by offering users approved foods with "consumable" and "lean and green" meal instructions.

Social support is an essential element for the success of any weight loss program.

Overall this diet has been very good. For me, it was well worth the time and money. It was nice to have someone else plan my meals for me. I liked having specific goals and calorie targets each day. It worked well for my particular lifestyle and eating habits.

I hope you learned something!

Lightning Source UK Ltd.
Milton Keynes UK
UKHW020812170621
385664UK00001B/237